I Have Music

Dona Herweck Rice

Library of Congress Cataloging-in-Publication Data

Names: Rice, Dona, author.
Title: I have music / Dona Herweck Rice.
Description: Huntington Beach, CA : Teacher Created Materials, 2018. | Description based on print version record and CIP data provided by publisher; resource not viewed.
Identifiers: LCCN 2018020234 (print) | LCCN 2018021473 (ebook) | ISBN 9781493898961 () | ISBN 9781493898220 (pbk.)
Subjects: LCSH: Musical instruments--Juvenile literature.
Classification: LCC ML460 (ebook) | LCC ML460 .R515 2018 (print) | DDC 784.19--dc23
LC record available at https://lccn.loc.gov/2018020234

Publishing Credits

Rachelle Cracchiolo, M.S.Ed., *Publisher*
Conni Medina, M.A.Ed., *Managing Editor*
Nika Fabienke, Ed.D., *Content Director*
Véronique Bos, *Creative Director*
Shaun N. Bernadou, *Art Director*
Carol Huey-Gatewood, M.A.Ed., *Editor*
Valerie Morales, *Associate Editor*
Courtney Roberson, *Senior Graphic Designer*

Image Credits: All images from iStock and/or Shutterstock.

Teacher Created Materials
5301 Oceanus Drive
Huntington Beach, CA 92649-1030
www.tcmpub.com

ISBN 978-1-4938-9822-0

Printed by: 51497
Printed in: Taiwan

I have  .

sticks

I have  .

drums

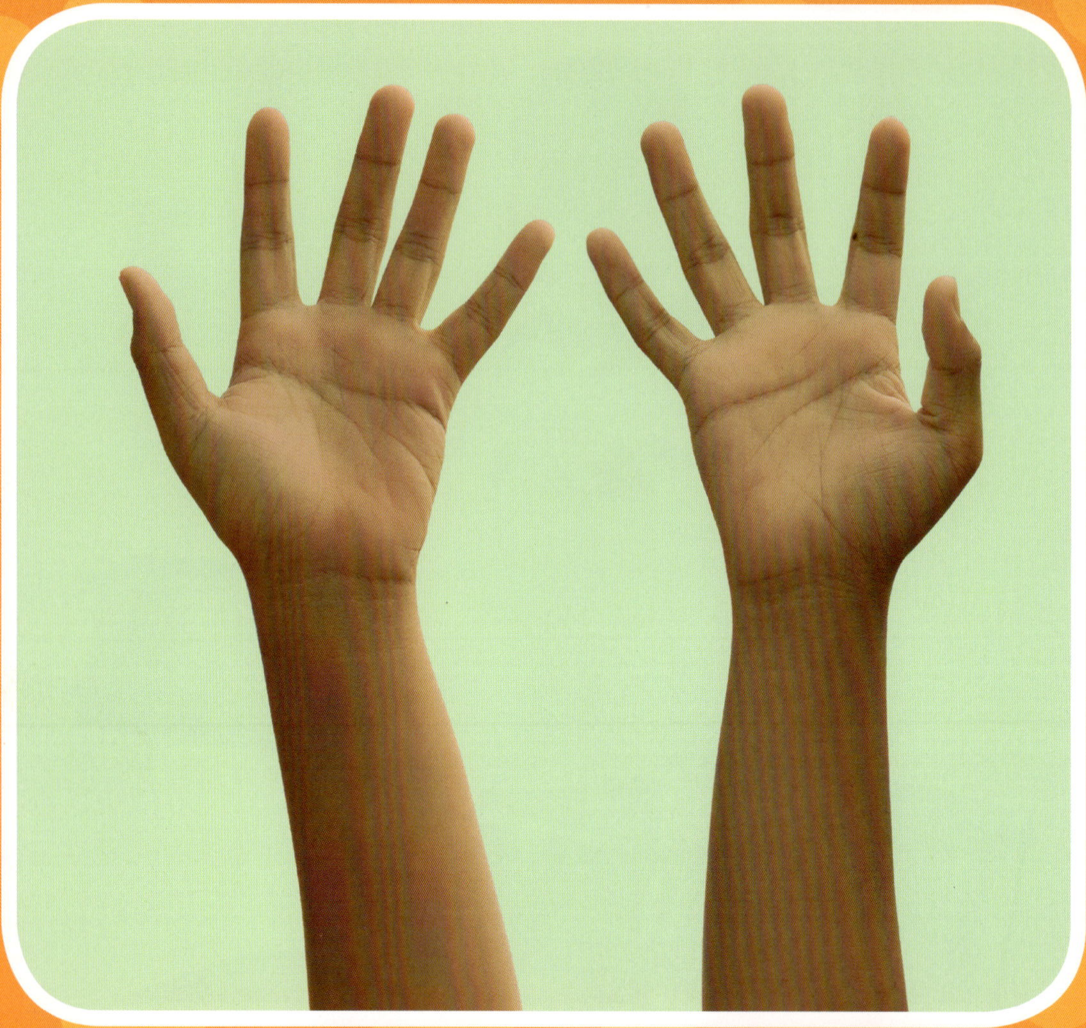

I have 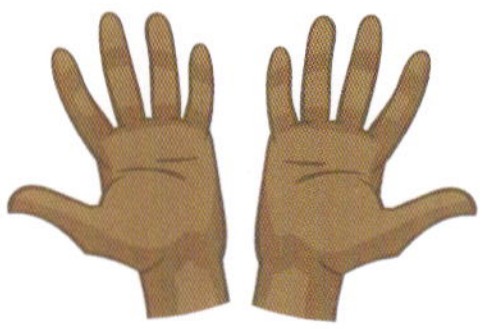 .

hands

I have .

bells

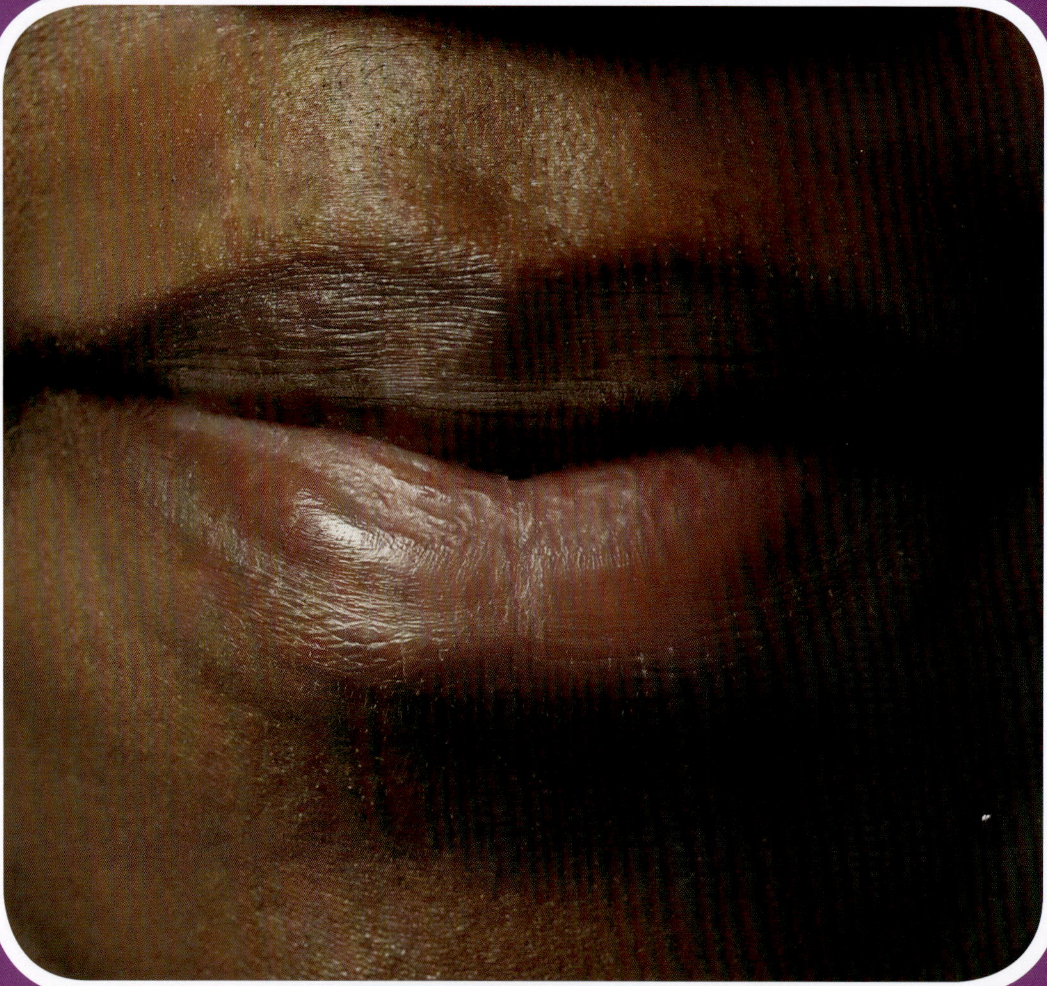

I have 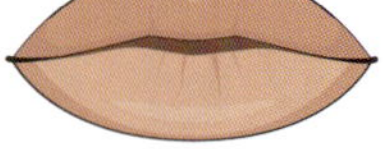 .

lips

I have .

horns

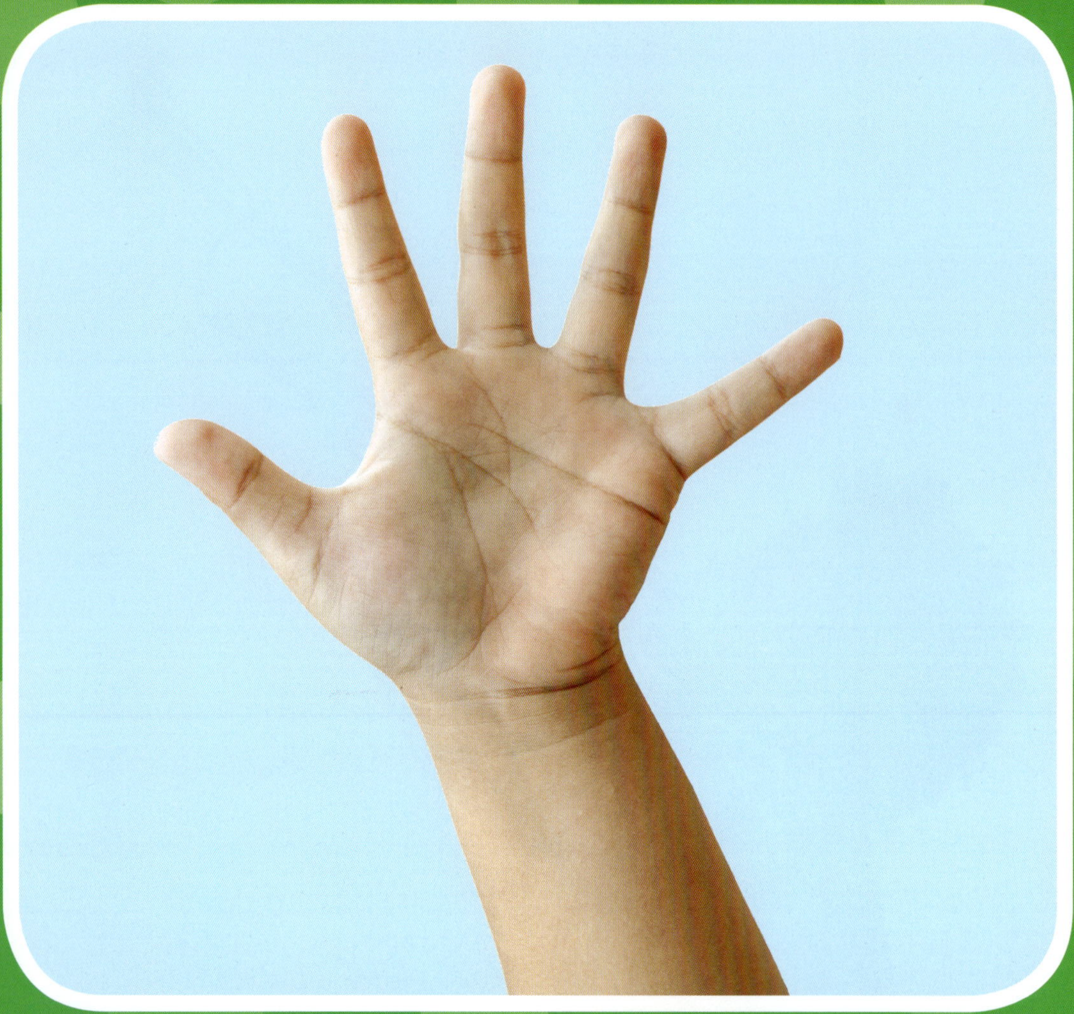

I have 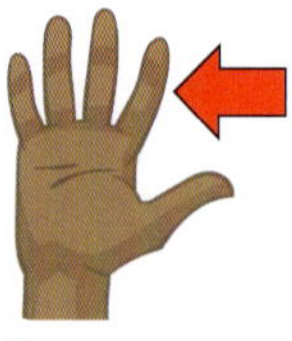 .

fingers

I have  .

keys

I have 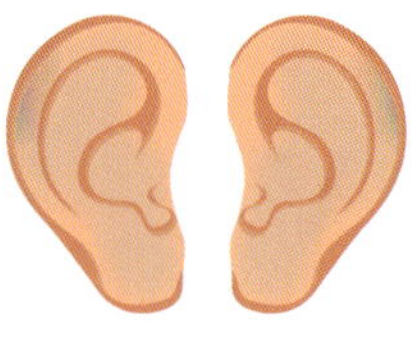 .

ears

I have  .

music

High-Frequency Words

have
I